John Stuart Blackie

The Constitutional Association on Forms of Government

A historical Review and Estimate of the Growth of the principal Types of

political etc.

John Stuart Blackie

The Constitutional Association on Forms of Government
A historical Review and Estimate of the Growth of the principal Types of political
etc.

ISBN/EAN: 9783337069520

Printed in Europe, USA, Canada, Australia, Japan

Cover: Foto ©Suzi / pixelio.de

More available books at **www.hansebooks.com**

THE CONSTITUTIONAL ASSOCIATION.

ON

FORMS OF GOVERNMENT:

A HISTORICAL REVIEW AND ESTIMATE OF THE GROWTH OF THE PRINCIPAL

TYPES OF POLITICAL ORGANISM IN EUROPE, FROM THE GREEKS

AND ROMANS DOWN TO THE PRESENT TIME.

A LECTURE,

DELIVERED IN THE FREE TRADE HALL, MANCHESTER, BY REQUEST OF THE

CONSTITUTIONAL ASSOCIATION, ON WEDNESDAY, APRIL 24, 1867,

BY

JOHN STUART BLACKIE, ESQ.,

PROFESSOR OF GREEK IN THE UNIVERSITY OF EDINBURGH.

LONDON:

WHITTAKER AND CO.

EDINBURGH: EDMONSTON AND DOUGLAS; MANCHESTER: J. HEYWOOD, DEANSGATE.

1867.

PRICE TWOPENCE.

THE CONSTITUTIONAL ASSOCIATION.

President.
W. R. CALLENDER, Jun., Esq., D.L., J.P., F.S.A.

Vice-Presidents.

The Right Hon. Earl of Dudley
The Hon. Algernon F. Egerton, M.P., D.L., J.P.
Charles Turner, Esq., M.P., D.L., J.P.
Lieutenant-Colonel Gray, M.P., D.L., J.P.
Edmund Buckley Esq., M.P.
W. Balliol Brett, Esq., Q.C., M.P.
T. Hornby Birley, Esq., Manchester
Sam Mendel, Esq., J.P., Manchester
George Walker, Esq., J.P., Manchester
Lieutenant-Colonel Edward Loyd, D.L., J.P., Lillesden, Hawkhurst, Kent
J. Smith Entwistle, Esq., D.C.L., M.A., D.L., J.P., Foxholes, Rochdale
John Munn, Esq., J.P., Manchester
Albert Hall, Esq., J.P., Stalybridge
John M. Kershaw, Esq., J.P., Ashton-under-Lyne
R. H. Norreys, Esq., D.L., J.P., Davyhulme Hall
William Gibb, Esq., D.L., J.P., Manchester
R. S. Sowler, Esq., Q.C., Manchester
Professor Blackie, Edinburgh
John Sudlow, Esq., Manchester
S. H. Norris, Esq., J.P., Altrincham
Thomas Brooks, Esq., St. Mawes
James Sewell, Esq., Manchester
William Bleackley, Esq., Prestwich
Ralph Hall, Esq., Manchester
Lieutenant-Colonel Deakin, Manchester
Charles Clarke, Esq., J.P., Manchester
Thos. Bazley Hall, Esq., J.P., Stalybridge
Peter Royle, Esq., M.D., J.P., Manchester
Captain J. Bennett, J.P., Manchester
B. St. J. B. Joule, Esq., J.P., Manchester
John Bennett, Esq., Willaston Hall, Nantwich
J. W. Maclure, Esq., J.P., Manchester
Fereday Smith, Esq., A.M., J.P., Manchester
Henry Gartside, Esq., Wharmton Tower, Saddleworth
George Peel, Esq., Manchester
Thomas Statter, Esq., Manchester
Lieutenant-Colonel Mellor, Brookfield, Ashton-under-Lyne
H. Howarth Vernon, Esq., M.D., J.P., Ashton-under-Lyne
Clement Hall, Esq., Manchester
James Bellhouse, Esq., Manchester
James Chadwick, Esq., Castleton
Charles A. Stewart, Esq., Manchester
Frederick Lowton Spinks, Esq., J.P., M.A., Serjeant-at-Law, Faversham
Arthur Birley, Esq., Whalley Range
J. B. Thorpe, Esq., Victoria Park
B Gray, Esq., Barrister-at-Law, Manchester
F. F. Whitehead, Esq., J.P., Saddleworth
J. H. Whitehead, Esq., J.P., Saddleworth
W. J. Harter, Esq., Manchester
William Rawstron, Esq., Manchester
Henry Sandford, Esq., Crow Croft Park
Captain Chas. Mercier, Manchester
Charles Baker Esq., J.P., Stockport
Major Bridgford, Manchester
E. O. Bleackley, Esq., Manchester
Captain R. Husband, Manchester
Thos. Potter, Esq., Barrister-at-Law, Manchester
Mr. Councillor Marshall, Manchester
Mr. Councillor Brown, Salford
Mr. Councillor William Booth, Manchester
Mr. Councillor Eastwood, Manchester
Mr. Councillor Livesley, Manchester
Mr. Councillor Anderton, Manchester
Mr. Councillor Grantham, Manchester
Mr. Councillor Charles Ashmore
W. H. Higgin, Esq., Barrister-at-Law, Manchester
William Saunders, Esq, Barrister-at-Law, Manchester
Thomas Jepson, Esq., Manchester
John Robinson, Esq., Manchester
David R. Davies, Esq., Manchester
Captain A. Crompton, Oldham
Hugh Higson, Esq., Manchester

Reuben Sims, Esq., Bedford, Leigh
Thomas Evans Lees, Esq., Oldham
George Thorpe, Esq., Old Trafford
James Hartley, Esq., Rochdale
Thomas Sowler, Esq., Manchester
Rev. W. Whitelegge, M.A., Manchester
Rev. J. E. Booth, M.A., Chorlton-cum-Hardy
Rev C. Marshall, M.A., Harpurhey
Rev. E. A. Lang, M.A., Manchester
Rev. W. R. Keeling, M.A., Blackley
Rev. Edward Parke, M.A., Blackley
Rev. George Edwards, M.A., Blackley
Rev. William Heffill, M.A., Dukinfield
Rev. W. Huntington, M.A., Cornbrook Park
Rev. F. O. Woodhouse, M.A., Hulme
Rev. Edward Owen, B.A., Oldham
Rev. C. Whittaker, M.A., Salford
Rev. Robt. Whittaker, M.A., Lees.
Robt. Whittaker, Esq., Walton-le-Dale
Rev. T. R. Busfield, M.A., Manchester
John Henry Law, Esq., Manchester
John M. Wike, Esq., Manchester
George Walker, Esq., M.D., Manchester
Barton Wood, Esq., Manchester
Henry Hall, Esq., Ashton-under-Lyne
John Moss, Esq., Manchester
S. P. Bidder, Esq., Manchester
Daniel Boote, Esq., Manchester
Wm. C. Chew, Esq., Lonsdale House, Lytham
Charles Oldham, Esq., Manchester
R. H. Gibson, Esq., Manchester
Thomas Dale, Esq., Manchester
N. P. Sandiford, Esq., Manchester
George Marsden, Esq., Manchester
Austin Shellard, Esq., Manchester
W. S. Sawyer, Esq., Manchester
Francis Baker, Esq., Stockport
J. D. Kennedy, Esq., Manchester
Thomas Preston, Esq., Manchester
W. D. B. Antrobus, Esq., Manchester
Henry Warburton, Esq., Harpurhey
Samuel Warburton, Esq., Harpurhey
Henry Warburton, jun., Esq., Harpurhey
James B. Thorpe, Esq., Manchester
Robert Andrew, Esq., Moston House
R. Mattley, Esq., Rochdale
John R. Baldwin, Esq., Rochdale
William Bradley, Esq., Stockport
J. Mc. Millan, Esq., Manchester
J. W. Walton, Esq., Manchester
E. W. Roylance, Esq., Manchester
J. W. Makin, Esq., Salford
Alfred Nicholls, Esq., Manchester
William Smith, Esq., Manchester
Henry Fisher, Esq., Manchester
Henry Keeling, Esq., Manchester
Alexander Mitchell, Esq., Manchester
A. K. Sidebottom, Esq., J.P., Mottram
John Cotterill, Esq., Manchester
J. H. Birley, Esq., Newton-le-Willows
Andrew Dobbie, Esq., Manchester
John Sowler, Esq., Manchester
Pookes Royle, Esq., Manchester
John Higgin Esq., Rochdale
Howarth Ashton, Esq., J.P., Prestwich
William Hanmer, Esq., Wilmslow
Captain Alfred Knowles, Manchester
S. Tweedale, Esq., Rochdale
Lawrence Rawstron, Esq., Manchester
J. Gardner, Esq., Manchester
H. C. Oats, Esq., Barrister-at-Law, Manchester
Wm. Smith, Esq., Collyhurst
E. H. Siddell, Esq., Manchester
W. W. Mc. Kay, Esq., Manchester
Jas. Watson, jun., Esq., Manchester
John J. Wood Esq., Manchester
Robt. Stewart, Esq., Manchester
Jas. Broughton, Esq., Higher Broughton
Mr. Councillor Farmer, Salford
Major H. Fishwick, Rochdale
Nicholas Kilvert, Esq., Whalley Range

OBJECTS OF THE ASSOCIATION.

Firstly.—To counteract by all lawful means the influence of any popular
agitations, the action of which may tend to the undue acquisition
of political power by any particular class of the people, and to the
ultimate evils arising from the usurpations of democracy.

Secondly.—It is proposed, by holding public meetings and by other
agencies, to induce among all classes such full and fair discussion of
political principles as may result in the most extended adoption of
correct views on Constitutional Government.

Thirdly.—To support Parliament in the free discharge of its legislative
functions, uninfluenced by any intimidation which may from time
to time be brought to bear upon its deliberations.

Fourthly.—The Association cordially supports such measures of Reform
in the representation of the people as—while preserving the present
Constitution of the country—shall admit to the privileges of the
Franchise all those, who from their industry and intelligence, may
fairly be judged competent to its proper exercise.

JAMES TAYLOR, } Hon. Secs.
M. H. CHADWICK, }

CHIEF OFFICE, 8, PARSONAGE,
BLACKFRIARS STREET, MANCHESTER.

Donations or subscriptions may be forwarded to the Treasurer, WM.
AMBROSE, Esq., Barrister-at-Law, 37, Cross-street, Manchester.

Members enrolled on payment of 1s. or upwards.

Meeting of the Constitutional Association,

AT THE FREE TRADE HALL, APRIL 24th, 1867.

ADDRESS BY PROFESSOR BLACKIE,

"ON FORMS OF GOVERNMENT."

Mr. CHARLES TURNER, M.P. for South Lancashire, presided, and there were also present on the platform: The Revs. W. Whitelegge, M.A., C. Whittaker, F. B. Wright, W. Huntington, W. Woodville ; Messrs. W. R. Callender, jun. (president of the Constitutional Association), Wm. Young, — Sanderson, W. Ambrose, T. Helsby, G. Scott (London), J. Collinge, R. Duckworth (secretary Conservative Club, Blackburn), J. B. Edge (Bolton), R. Hall, C. Hall, R. Udall, Captain Sawyer, Captain Knowles, Colonel Deakin, Captain Birley (Newton-le-Willows), W. Gibb (Swinton Park), J. B. Thorpe, Thomas Statter, Captain Evans Lees (Oldham), George Thorpe, Councillor Anderton, Councillor William Booth, James M'Millan, R. H. Norreys (Davyhulme Hall), Dr. Royle, R. Higgin, R. Mattley, Jas. Hartley (Rochdale), Thos. Dale, Alfred Higgins (Salford), George Slater, J. Palin (Liverpool), W. D. B. Antrobus, Edward Hull, S. P. Bidder, James Pilling (Rochdale), James Fletcher (Kearsley), Joseph Leech (Rochdale), James Pickering (Orrell), W. H. Harbottle (Wigan), J. F. Mart, Joseph Lowe (Salford). The large room was well filled.

The CHAIRMAN, who was received with great cheering, said : Ladies and gentlemen,—It is with very great pleasure that, at the request of the Constitutional Association, I take the chair this evening on the occasion of the delivery of a lecture by Professor Blackie on forms of government. (Applause.) The talent and ability of the learned Professor ensure to us a lecture at once interesting and instructive. A lecture delivered by an able man, and a man of information on such a subject, must always be, but particularly so at a period like the present, when the legislature of the country is engaged in remodelling the basis on which rests one of the most important parts of that form of government with which this country has been blessed for so long a period. (Applause.) In the re-construction of our electoral body, I trust that that balance of the different interests and classes of the community will be preserved, which, while the basis of the House of Commons is extended, will make that body continue to be what it has hitherto been, a fair representation of every portion of the community. (Hear, hear.) Gentlemen, though this lecture is delivered at the instance of the Constitutional Association, I don't take it that this meeting is a political one, in the strict sense of the word. (Hear, hear.) But, at the same time, called as it is at the instance of the Constitutional Association, I think that I am justified in considering that it is a Conservative meeting. (Hear, hear, and applause.)

And treating it as a Conservative meeting—as a meeting called by an association which has for its object to preserve the constitution of the country in Church and State—(hear, hear)—as against the objects of those societies which, however they may disguise it, have for their ultimate design the uprooting of those institutions under which we have so long lived, and under which this country has enjoyed so much liberty. I may say that a reform in Parliament is, I think, on all hands held now to be a political necessity, and I trust and believe that whatever alteration is made in the constitution of the electoral body will be at once liberal and conservative. (Applause.) I think we are all agreed that it is most desirable to extend the franchise to the more intelligent and industrious of the working classes of the community. (Hear, hear.) Well, then, the great object we have in view is to ascertain how that is to be done, and in my opinion the measure proposed by the Government will have that effect—will at the same time be more liberal and more conservative than any measure which has yet been proposed. (Applause.) In private life—and the same thing extends to public life—when we want a steady, honest, industrious man, we look to the man who pays his way and discharges all his obligations, both public and private. (Applause.) Without entering more fully into this subject, which would occupy too much time—for I am only here to-night for the purpose of taking the chair, and I will make but a few introductory observations—my own feeling is, and I am happy to find that the meeting agrees with it—that the best test that we can have in introducing the working men into the suffrage is to bring in the industrious, the sober and honest working man, and keep out the idle,- the dissolute and the thriftless working man. (Applause.) The one we all want to admit, and the other we all want to exclude, and for that purpose we must have some test, and the best, I repeat it, is to choose the man who discharges both his public and private obligations and pays his way, and exclude the man who does neither. (Hear, hear, and applause.) I am not here, as I said before, for the purpose of making a speech, nor are you here for the purpose of listening to me, but we are all here for the purpose of listening to a lecture which the learned professor has been kind enough to come here to deliver ; and with these few remarks I call upon him to deliver that lecture. (Applause.)

Professor BLACKIE, who was received with loud and continued applause, in introducing his lecture, said :—It may appear strange that a Greek Professor from Edinburgh should come to talk politics in the great cotton capital of the south. It does appear to me more strange that I should have come here and be standing upon this platform at all. (Laughter.) I am sure that the gentlemen who asked me to come here will bear me witness that I was very slow in answering to their invitation. Like a true Scot, I was very cautious before I entered upon it. Like an old trout, I took a whole week to consider whether I would bite or not, and at last I did bite—(hear, hear, and laughter)—because I found that they did not make any very hard conditions. They did not bind me down to any political creed. (Applause.) I understood only that they were champions for the British constitution—the very name of the association showed that —(applause)—and I also knew perfectly well, too well, from the tone of various public speeches, and of various popular magazines or journals that were sent about, that there was a party in this country that whatever they chose to say, or however they chose to mince their profession, were in their hearts, in their arguments, and in their principles, hostile to the British constitution; and, at the present moment, desired to Americanise the whole of the social organism of the country. (Hear, hear, and cries of "Shame.") I had therefore no doubt whatever in accepting this invitation. And it does not appear so very absurd that a professor of Greek should lecture upon a political question. My great countryman, Adam Smith, though no merchant, wrote about free trade in corn before ever Richard Cobden was heard or even dreamt about— and it may be possible that I, who am merely a political thinker, may have some ideas not unworthy of being considered by you, who are readers in the great practical world of politics. I therefore shall take you altogether out of your local questions and temporary disputes, even to that grand point of view,—the historic. (Hear, hear.) I must take you back to a time when it might be difficult to discern Manchester upon the face of the map. We will take, my friends, a review of three or four thousand years, in comparison with which the question of Mr. Disraeli's Reform Bill or that of Mr. Gladstone either is a very small matter. We shall endeavour to lay down large principles which are, or at least which ought to be, included in all reform bills which are being brought about just now. (Hear, hear.) Now I am quite aware—I know that the English people don't like metaphysics—Scotchmen like an argument, and Englishmen like facts—(laughter and applause)—therefore I will give my arguments altogether in the shape of facts, and I will bring forward before you the main lines of six of the greatest constitutions that have been in the history of the world. (Hear, hear.) Looking upon them as political experiments, I will tell you what they have done—I will show you how they failed, and how they have fallen. Those six constitutions are the constitutions of Sparta, of Athens, of Rome, these three from ancient times; and then from the modern times I will take three, namely, the constitutions of Prussia, of America, and of Great Britain. I take these six, partly because they afford the most excellent contrast—partly because they are the most final in the history of the world—and partly because I happen to know most about them. (Hear, hear, and laughter.) If you ask me what I know about Prussia, I had the happiness of living there two or three years of my life. I can see how its constitution works, and I speak as a man who knows something about it. The Professor further said that he should be satisfied if, as the result of his lecture, he could get the people to study for themselves. It would be much better for them than attending to John Bright, or any of those travelling demagogues—(applause)—or listening to their speeches which were full of vituperation and passion, and little else. (Laughter.) He quite admitted that Mr. Bright was sometimes right—(hear, hear)— but by no means always. The learned Professor then proceeded with his lecture, and said :—

Mr. Chairman, Ladies, and Gentlemen,—There are four great errors in reference to the philosophy of politics which we see not uncommonly committed, when judgments are delivered on different forms of government. The first and most vulgar is to think all forms of government bad except that under which we have the fortune to live, to mirror ourselves in our own perfections, and to ignore the excellencies of our neighbour. The second is the reverse of this, to fix our regards only on the thorns of our own position, and to see nothing but roses in that of our neighbour. The third is to attribute to forms of government sins or virtues which belong not to any form of government in particular, but to human nature in general, and to half-a-dozen peculiarities, in climate, race, genius, culture, situation, personality, which defy all measurement and transcend all calculation; and the fourth is to fling all political analogies and precedents overboard with a heroic scepticism, and launch out into the great sea of social possibilities with no direction but that which has its root in enormous self-confidence, and a chivalrous trust in the chapter of accidents. The mere statement of these fallacies may be considered sufficient for their refutation : nevertheless, the page of history and the atmosphere of political ideas is full of facts and fancies that can be traced distinctly to hasty and inconsiderate reasoning on one of these insufficient postulates. By proceeding on the first postulate, British statesmen have forced British forms of constitutional government on peoples who had neither the knowledge nor the training necessary for their success; and American statesmen may some day find it necessary to make war on the British possessions in America, in order that no part of that extensive continent may lack the inestimable blessing of a republican government. By arguing from the second assumption, certain politicians in this country of well-tempered monarchy, aristocracy, and democracy, have convinced themselves that there is no hope for the world except in the universal adoption of that form of government whose great merit is that it happens to be exactly the reverse in all points of that to which they have been accustomed. Every man knows where his own shoe pinches, and nothing is more obvious than to imagine that your neighbour's shoe does not pinch at all because he has no corn exactly upon the same place of the same toe. It is the easiest of all things to admire your neighbour's house, because it possesses some beauties that cannot be predicated of yours : a fine open situation, a gracefully-proportioned front, a sunny exposure ; for, so long as you do not live in the house, you cannot know that it is ill-drained, that the wind roars in the chimneys, that the adjacent marshes breed mosquitoes and malaria, that there is dry rot in the wood, and that the roof lets in the rain. No man knows a woman till he marries her ; and those who, at the distance of the whole swell of the Atlantic, delight to indulge their fancy in contemplating the blessedness of men who live under a democratic polity, might lightly alter their opinions by only a few years' experience of the low intrigues, the blushless lies, the rampant selfishness, and the incalculable corruption of all kinds that grow out of the dung-bed of a presidential election. An instance of false political judgment arising out of the third assumption, we find in the case of those who ascribe to democracy all the bloody and savage excesses of the French revolution ; when those excesses arose partly out of the Celtic temperament, partly out of the very nature of all violent revolutions, and belonged as certainly to an oligarchic revolution in ancient Athens, as to a democratic one in modern Paris. The fourth postulate is hastily assumed by those

who are too ignorant to recognise, too lazy to investigate, or too dogmatic
to tolerate the grave lessons of political experience ; it suits their indo-
lence, or the party purpose which spurs them, to refuse instruction from
far times or from distant places ; and therefore they career along with
a gay confidence in their own conceit, saying that all historical parallels
are fallacious. But the lessons of history in reference to political science
are not the less valuable because they require to be used with dis-
crimination ; and the parading an accidental difference will not, any more
than in other branches of science, nullify the common laws which have
their root in a fundamental identity. I, for one, believe the lessons
derivable from political experience to be as certain as any that belong to
the most exact sciences ; the only source of disturbance in political
science being that, when parties are engaged in a struggle for political
power, they are not in a humour to seek for political truth, and therefore
fail to find it. But while the parties directly engaged are mostly incapable of judgment, the impartial spectator may often estimate the forces
and predict the results as certainly as any calculation in a dynamical
or mechanical equation. Moral forces may not be measurable exactly
in inches ; but they are measurable.

With these convictions, and having been requested by the office-
bearers of this influential association to deliver a lecture that shall
contain such deductions from the rich political experience of centuries
as may be useful at the present important crisis of our constitutional
history, I proceed to place before you some of the grand political experiments that have been made or are being made in the world. I shall
select three from the ancient and three from the modern world, exhibit-
ing types as diverse and as contrasted as possible. Leaving the East
out of view, which for various reasons presents no parallels by which we
can profit, I shall cast a glance in the ancient world, at the forms of
government in Sparta, Athens, and Rome ; while in the modern world I
shall confine myself to Prussia, America, and Great Britain. The subject
is a broad one ; and you will, therefore, be content if I bring before you
only the grand outlines of the picture, and deduce a few of the most
general and the most incontrovertible propositions.

SPARTA.

The original form of government in all the Greek states, was, as
Aristotle informs us, monarchical. The general prevalence of this form
of polity, not only in early Greece but all over the world, is easily
explained. The first thing wanted in all society is unity of action and
consistent adherence to a common plan ; and as the greatest obstacle to
this is the spirit of individualism and the tendency of great masses of
men to split into parties, which makes co-operation difficult, the obvious
remedy is found in submission to the supreme authority of a single
dominant will. This enforced subordination, useful in peace, becomes
necessary in war ; and as in the early stages of society hostile encounters
are so common as to become a recognised part of every man's life, the
common type of early governments is monarchical. It is obvious, however, that the constraint thus implied cannot be agreeable to the persons
who submit to it : they accept it as a necessity rather than delight in

it as a fact. For the natural form of government in the earliest stages of society is not monarchical, but aristocratic. Masses of men gather under the leadership of those commanding individuals whom talent, hereditary resources, family connections, or local advantages point out as the natural governors of particular districts. Thus instead of one king we have many to start with; and, as these have equal rights among themselves, it is manifest that they will be inclined to look upon a supreme king as an encroachment on their natural rights, and will regard his office as a sort of prolonged dictatorship, not to be tolerated longer than necessary. This position of the early Greek kings towards the early Greek aristocracy is evident enough on the face of the Homeric poems and in the whole plot of the Iliad. Agamemnon was King of the Greeks only so long as the war of Troy lasted; after the fall of the god-built walls we hear no more of a King of Greece, or even a general-in-chief of the Greeks, till the time of Alexander the Great: we have only the lords of the Spartan, Argive, and Attic districts, who become supreme kings each in his own domain. But even these local kingships were not destined to last. The provincial king is only first among a large family of peers, who watch his proceedings with jealousy and are ready to lay hold of his first abuse of supreme power, as an excuse, in the name of right and equality, for re-establishing the authority of the national aristocracy. This is the secret of the overthrow of the kingly power in the most distinguished states of Greco-Roman antiquity. Only one notable state escaped this contagion. This state was SPARTA; and even here we find the power of the kings limited in the most signal manner, not only by the general strength of the aristocratic element in the constitution, but by the curious accident, or rather cunning device, of the double kingship; a device than which nothing could be more effective as a means of securing the preponderance of aristocratic influence in the state, nothing more ridiculous, if it was intended to give the monarchical element in the constitution fair play. Notwithstanding this unfavourable position of the monarchs, however, the kings of Sparta, either by the weight of their general character, as in the case of Agesilaus, or by their position as generals-in-chief at the head of a warlike nation, maintained much more real power to the last than at the present moment belongs to our constitutional sovereign. We have, therefore, in Sparta the only example of a mixed monarchy analogous to the British constitution among the prominent states of Greek and Roman antiquity. For besides the aristocratic assembly called γερουσία, or Council of the Elders, they had the ἐκκλησία, or general assembly, as we see it convened by Telemachus in the second book of the Odyssey, and as we find it afterwards in Athens in the exercise of all the legislative and executive functions of the state.

Now, what are the political lessons which a consideration of the rise and fall of the famous Spartan monarchy ought to teach the political thinkers of the present day? First, we learn that the grand principle of stability and permanence in political institutions is a national, healthy, strong, and well ordered aristocracy. The other states of Greece, without the stable element of the kingship, supported by a strong natural aristocracy, that is, in the case of the Spartan γερουσία, a House of Lords continually recruited from the

great and the most tried men of the people, and holding their dignity for life
—the other states of Greece, I say, lost all sense of social security in the
shifting ascendancy of opposing factions ; and in the midst of this weary
and bloody turmoil Sparta stood forth alone as the model of stable
government, admired not less by practical politicians like Thucydides
than by speculative philosophers like Plato. But Sparta owed this permanence, like Rome, not merely to its aristocratic institutions, but to its
military discipline and the habits of order and subordination which military discipline necessarily implies. In one sentence, therefore, let us
say that the strength of Sparta lay in its aristocratic government limited
by monarchy, and in its habits of military discipline; and of these ex-
cellences the first unquestionably is shared with it by Great Britain.
But there were sources of weakness deeply seated in the constitution of
that country which ultimately led to its ruin. Lacedæmon had no sound
basis of popular energy and enterprise out of which the upper strata of
society could be largely recruited : the ancient Spartans, like the modern
Turks, were an army of strangers encamped among a conquered people
whom they had reduced to slavery and kept in the most hated bondage.
A Spartan army was not easily beaten ; but when beaten, it had nothing
to fall back on. The Spartans were like the Southerns in the late American
war : they were conquered not for want of manhood, but for want of
men. Hence we learn the great lesson, that without a free, independent,
and enterprising population no nation can achieve the highest greatness.
The Spartans and Messenians were exactly in the same relation as the
Turks in those parts of the empire where the population is composed mainly of Greeks ; or as Great Britain would be if the whole
British population were Irish Catholics, kept in social bondage by the
dominant minority of a Protestant aristocracy. The fundamental cause
of the fall of Sparta, therefore, is an open secret which any man may
read. It fell mainly because it wanted the root of democratic energy,
out of which alone a strong aristocracy can be sustained. Of the other
vices in its constitution I shall say nothing. The one-sidedness of its
military education has been noted by Aristotle ; and the dark deeds of
its unscrupulous oligarchy have been largely exposed by Mr. Grote. To
us happily it affords few lessons which may not be more effectively learned
from the grander polity of Rome. Of this anon. But the chronological
sequence demands that in this place first we enquire what lessons are to
be derived from the most brilliant of the ancient Greek states, that state
which in every higher sense to the world at large means Greece, viz.,

ATHENS.

Of this state, as every schoolboy knows—who has not heard of
Codrus? — the original polity was monarchical. The reasons above
stated, whatever the mythical account of the matter may be, led step
by step to the constitution of the most celebrated, the most brilliant, but
also one of the most short-lived democracies that the history of the
world presents. By the jealousy of the Attic aristocracy, kings were
first changed into archons for life, archons for life yielded to decennial
archons, and decennial archons became at last annual, with no high executive authority, but only judicial functions and recognized social position

The first great name in the more recent history of Athens is Solon, B.C. 600. This great legislator found the mass of the people suffering under oppression of the most grievous sort, which had arisen out of the long continued exclusive rule of the aristocracy, unchecked either by kingly control from above or popular power from below. For there is no maxim of political science more certain than that every privileged body, exercising for a long time supreme power without check is sure to abuse that power : there will grow up what we call a one-sided class legislation by which the unprivileged classes will feel themselves aggrieved. This state of things Solon found in Athens, and it is his immortal glory to have put an end to it by the sole weight of his wisdom and his character. Happy the people who in a great popular crisis have a great man to rely on ; happier still if they can discern the great man when he is there, and submit themselves to him, as the feeble ought always to do to the strong, the bad to the good, and the foolish to the wise! Solon not only settled the law of debtor and creditor, which in ancient Athens, as in ancient Rome, was on a most iniquitous footing, but he balanced, or did the best he could to achieve a balance between the old aristocratic and the young democratic elements in the constitution of such a nature as seemed best calculated to perpetuate both the reasonable influence of the one, and the just claims of the other. This constitution consisted of a court of the highest aristocratic dignity, called the Court of the Areopagus, of a senate or βουλή, answering to the γερουσία of Sparta, and an ἐκκλησία or popular assembly. Of the exact constitution and character of the Areopagus in those most ancient times, as well as of the character and position of the Solonian Senate, we are most imperfectly informed ; but are fairly entitled to conclude that both these bodies originally possessed an aristocratic character, and exercised an aristocratic influence, which within a very short period altogether disappeared. Certain it is that no people long trained to aristocratic supremacy bounds to extreme democracy by a leap ; and we shall not be surprised, therefore, to find the first great democratic movement against the mixed constitution contemplated by Solon made by Clisthenes in the year 510 B.C., the epoch of the Roman Tarquins, inspired with irresistible strength by the maritime element which decided the Great Persian War 480 B.C., and crowned with the cornice of completeness by the strong hands of Pericles in the generation immediately following. From this time, say 460 B.C. to the Battle of Chæronea, and the extinction of Greek independence by Philip of Macedon in the year 338, there prevailed in Athens a democracy of the most free and unfettered description. In this democracy the sole sovereignty lay in the assembly of the people ; the Senate was only a standing committee of their number ; the authority of the Court of Areopagus became merely honorary and judicial. What then did it achieve ? How did it work ? And why was it of so limited duration ? These are interesting questions which admit of being answered with the utmost distinctness and precision. But first let me make two important remarks which are absolutely necessary to any intelligible view of this subject. The Athenian democracy was not a democracy of household suffrage, or of manhood suffrage, in the sense in which our Radicals use these words ; or as these words become facts

i

iu the Pandemouian rabblement which rules New York. Every free-
born Athenian of full blood, and at some periods also of half blood, was
a voter in the ἐκκλησία. But these free Athenians were not above 20,000
in a population of 450,000, all the rest being children, women, and slaves.
On common occasions it was difficult to get 6,000 people to assemble in
the Pnyx for the transaction of public business. Now although this
assembly of a few thousand citizens of course included all classes of
people, it cannot be doubted that it excluded the great mass of that
lowest and most degraded class which universal suffrage admits in New
York, and would admit according to the theories of the American party
in this country. As compared with the democratic ideal which New
York has attained, and which our extreme democratic schemers hope to
attain, the constituency of Athens was a most select body. The second
remark that I have to make is, that it is a great fallacy to imagine that
the brilliant exhibition of intellect which was the glory of Greece' had
anything to do with the democratic form of government under which
Attic political influence attained its zenith. Some of the most renowned
names in Greek literature belong to ages and centuries with which
Athenian democracy had nothing to do. Homer, Thales, Pythagoras,
and Herodotus were all ·Asiatics. What produced that magnificent
efflorescence of human thought, which we call Greek literature,
was first the peculiar gift of God to that people, and second
the possession of that amount of popular freedom which is necessary
for the happy evolution of all moral and intellectual energy. But
it is a mistake to suppose that the liberty of any people has
anything to do with a democratic form of government. There is no
country in which more real personal, moral, and intellectual liberty
is enjoyed than Great Britain ; and we have produced a national literature which in most respects vies with, and in some respects surpasses,
the highest literature of ancient Greece. The star of Shakespeare
rose when the monarchy was still the most marked feature of our
mixed constitution. Cowper and Burns, Byron and Scott, Wordsworth and Tennyson, expanded the iridescent plumage of their
fine conceptions, under what Radicals call the "cold shade of aristocracy." Nay, even under the petty princedoms of Germany, before
the great uprising of popular energy in the year 1813, the greatest
literature was produced that has thrown a light over Europe since
the days of Shakespeare and Lord Bacon. Let the Athenian democracy, therefore, get full credit for its political achievements, but not
for fruit which grew in gardens which it never watered. What its
achievements were is shortly said. The great virtue of all democracies is energy and enterprise : indomitable and lofty enterprise is
what all impartial men admire in the democracy of Athens. The
deliverance of eastern Europe from the yoke of Oriental despotism, and
the sovereignty of the Greek race in Ægean seas maintained for a long
period against Persian tyranny, may fairly be considered as the two
great social results from Athenian democracy, for which the world can
never cease to be grateful. The answer to the second question, how
the government worked ? will, I am afraid, prove less satisfactory.
No doubt it was better in all respects than the government of self-

constituted local autocrats—such as Pisistratus and Dionysius—with
which it stood contrasted ; better in most respects than the aristocratic
government of Sparta ; not indeed because that government contained
the aristocratic element, but because the aristocracy there rested, as we
have seen, on no popular basis : but, in spite of its brilliancy, a cool
judge will say that it was a bad form of government, and, moreover, that
notwithstanding its comparatively select character, it was ruined in a
remarkably brief period precisely by those vices, which essentially belong
to an unmixed democratic constitution. It fell by one great fault and
two great sins, by the insolence of unbridled energy, by faction and by
corruption. The imperiousness of popular conceit sent Nicias to Syracuse
just as the haughtiness of military absolutism, in these latter days, brought
Napoleon to Moscow ; and both found a grave where they had hoped to
grasp a crown ; for "before honour comes humility"; and moderation,
which despotism and democracy alike disown, is the only safe guardian
of power. As for the faction and corruption, which are a neverfailing
growth from the rank soil of pure democracy, how effectually they com-
pleted the work of exhaustion, which the struggles of the Peloponnesian
war had commenced, the orations of Demosthenes sufficiently declare.
Had the Athenians acted with as much vigour against the petty barbaric
king of Pella, as one hundred and forty years before they had exhibited
against the great king of the East, the Macedonian captain never could
have set foot south of Mount Olympus ; but a century and a half of
unlimited democratic energy had done its perfect work ; a general
popular langour, the national legacy of over-exertion, had left the people
a willing prey to the hireling vendors of smooth lies, by whom they
were habitually surrounded. A single Demosthenes pleaded powerfully for a decided exhibition of the ancient energy : the people
came at last to his repeated call, but they came too late; and
one bloody battle laid their brilliant democracy helpless at the
feet of a barbarian autocrat, from whose country, as Demosthenes has it,
a few years before, they would not even have thought it reputable to
purchase a slave ! Such, so far as Athens is concerned, seem
to me to have been the main causes of her lamentable fall.
But there was another cause altogether external to the Athenian Constitution which enabled Philip, in a short career of conquest, to spread
the net of his bondage so successfully round every Greek State. This
other cause, however, is only another leaf from the same large chapter
of democratic dissention, which occupies so large a space in the book of
the world's history. The relation of the States of Greece to one another
was thoroughly democratic. They had a common language, a common
religion, and a common literature ; but they had no national unity.
Had there been such a thing as a Greek kingdom, and a King of Greece,
Philip of Macedon would never have been heard of on the large stage
of history, any more than the petty dynasts who sat on that rough
northern throne before him. Greece was subjugated by Macedonia,
because the parts of Greece hung as loosely together as the extreme
democratic policy of Calhoun would have made the states of America
hang together. An aggregate of perfectly independent states cannot
exist together long without war : in politics neighbours are always

cuemies; and so the Greek states in their mad rage for separate equality
and independence—what they called *autonomy*—exhausted their strength
in hereditary jealousies, and ever-reviving feuds; and thus an adroit enemy
by playing them off cunningly one against the other, though decidedly
inferior in strength to any two of them taken together, became in the
end easily the master of the whole. Thus ended that insane rage for
liberty and equality (but without fraternity) among the energetic Greek
people, of which the seed wherever it appears is always insolence and the
fruit slavery.—A thousand years' servitude is certainly a very heavy
price to pay for a hundred years of the most unfettered liberty.

ROME.

The order of time now brings us to the Romans, the great soldiers,
statesmen, and lawyers of antiquity. The Roman constitution presents
a medium between the one-sided aristocracy of Sparta and the one-sided
democracy of Athens. Its cradle, like that of both the great Greek
states, was monarchical : but while in Sparta the kingship remained with
a divided but not therefore ineffective personality, in Rome it was violently
expelled, and its very name became the shibboleth of national abhor-
rence. In Rome the government was at first so much the more aristocratic than at Sparta, as there was no king to divide the honours or the
authority of the state with the closely banded strength of the patrician
interest ; but there was a people in Rome instead of a population of
helots, and this people gradually grew in strength, and knew to assert
its rights so powerfully, that in the full aspect of its manhood the
Roman polity might well be described as a strong aristocracy moderately
tempered by popular rights. In this respect it presents a striking
analogy to the British constitution as it existed before the Reform Bill
of 1832 ; and indeed, if the Roman aristocracy had been wise enough to
retain their king, they might have boasted a constitution that, in its
whole history, would have presented a close parallel to our own. Even
as it is, there is no state in whose fortunes so much of British constitutional history lies prefigured as in ancient Rome. The Roman senate
was a body composed of three hundred of the most honourable and well-
tried members of the state, belonging principally to aristocratic families,
and holding their seats for life. Our own House of Lords and our
House of Commons melted into one, and constantly recruited by elections
made in a popular assembly under strong aristocratic influences, would
give a pretty accurate idea of the Roman Senate. As in Sparta so in
Rome, the real governing power lay in this aristocratic House of
Commons ; and it was this aristocratic preponderance, combined as
in Sparta with stern habits of military discipline, and with what
Sparta did not possess, a sturdy and orderly yeomanry, to which Rome
owed its victory over the Etruscans, the Samnites, the Gauls, and the
Carthaginians, and the establishment of a polity that was commensu-
rate with the girth of the civilized world. But this form of government,
though successful as an engine of conquest and control, was in
its internal arrangements very far from perfect. The unity and central
strength which the presence of a king might more fitly have imparted
was supplied by the compact adhesiveness of the aristocracy; and the

danger arising from the annual struggle for the double consulship could only be staved off so long as the aristocracy were strong enough to direct the popular elections, and wise enough not to quarrel among themselves. But popular power was always growing, and a wider field was always opening up for personal ambition among the candidates for the consulship; and, worst of all, manners were being more and more corrupted by the enormous influx of wealth from the subjugated dependencies in the East: all these influences made the wise preponderance of a patriotic aristocracy in the course of a few centuries impossible, and the aristocratic constitution of Rome was, by the agency of democratic violence, changed to a military despotism within five hundred years after the expulsion of the kings. The history of this overthrow of so famous a polity, in which Polybius and the Romanized Greeks saw so many elements of excellence, is exceedingly instructive. It was to the democratic element that aristocratic Rome finally succumbed. The form in which a democracy always asserts its power is faction; and faction is never more potent than when democracy has to assert its position and gain its triumphs in the face of a powerful aristocracy. Now this was exactly the situation of affairs in ancient Rome. So long as the constitution stood, it stood by virtue of a wise balance of parties; when it fell, it fell by a disturbance of that balance; and the men who ultimately succeeded in laying the yoke of permanent servitude on the whole people, mounted into power borne forward on the big wave of democratic passion and applause. How came this about? First of all by the fault of the aristocracy themselves. They were strong enough for a firm government, but too strong for a just government. Their grasp of power had been too close, and their lease too long, to allow of their treating the rights of the increasing commons with that generous sympathy which they deserved. The consequence was—as it always must be under such circumstances—the creation of demagogues, and the inauguration of schemes, which, when once cherished, could not end otherwise than in the overthrow of the governing power, and the introduction of a despot under the guise of a demagogue. In the principal popular assembly, that in which the highest magistrates were elected, the aristocracy had always asserted a more than equitable influence: and it was to counteract this that the tribunes, or deans of the people, as we may perhaps call them, made it their object always more and more to extend the jurisdiction of the *comitia tributa*—an assembly of the people of purely democratic constitution, and entirely under the control of the demagogues or popular leaders of the hour. The result of this continual striving was that in year 286 before Christ — just about the time when the Ptolemies were founding their famous lettered monarchy in Alexandria,—one Hortensius, a noble of plebeian extraction, during a season of great popular discontent got a bill passed which gave the democratic assembly of the tribes voting by universal suffrage unlimited power to make laws independently of the senate. From that moment an *imperium in imperio* was created, under the operation of which no constitution could stand, much less a constitution which depended so completely for its existence on the balance of opposing and yet co-operating parties as that of Rome. The doom of the city was from that moment fixed. The severe ordeal of the Punic wars prevented the great internal schism of which the seed was thus sown from bursting into blossom, for more than a century; but shortly after that vital danger was outlived, the great contest between the aristocracy and the democracy broke out, which ended, as such contests almost invariably do, in the overthrow of popular liberty. The immediate occasion to this terrible struggle sprung, as might have been expected, out of the undue preponderance of the aristocracy. When the population of Italy was comparatively thin, a great part of the land which had been conquered by the Romans, naturally fell into the hands of the already existing proprietors of the old families who could most conveniently manage it. Nevertheless, their legal position in reference to this public land was that only of occupancy; they had no right of ownership, and the State might at any time reclaim the usufruct which it had allowed. But there is nothing so difficult in the execution of social justice as the reclamation of possessory rights which have been allowed to lie dormant. The consequence was that when the first of the Gracchi, a noble of the Whig or Liberal party as we would phrase it, in the year 133 B.C. brought forward a measure for dividing the public lands amongst the people, and creating a class of small proprietors to counter-balance the over-growth of the aristocracy, the internecine war between the now hostile elements of the State commenced with a decision and a savageness of which only Romans were capable, and ended, after a century of the most terrible deluge of bitterness and blood, in the establishment of an unlimited despotism by Augustus Cæsar. The details of this sanguinary struggle furnish the most awful warning of the terrible results that must always follow, when a violent and excited democratic assembly is brought into direct collision with a strong and a determined aristocracy. Each will naturally assert supremacy in its own sphere, and where passion receives no counsels of compromise from reason, Force comes in as the divine arbiter. It is always difficult in such cases to apportion the blame among the parties. In the matter of the Agrarian laws the aristocracy was confessedly wrong; but the palliation of their offence lay in this that they were acting defensively against what, from their point of view, they could not but regard as an unwarranted aggression on their prescriptive rights; and the real blame of initiating the long career of civil violence in which the history of Rome thenceforth consisted, lay neither with the demagogic Gracchi, nor with their aristocratic antagonists, but with that rash Reform Bill of 286, which we have mentioned, called the *lex Hortensia*, constituting a purely democratic assembly, with paramount authority, right in the face of the supreme legislative and executive council of the state. Such an assembly, especially in an age of increasing wealth, luxury, and corruption, could not but be used as a stepping-stone in the march of ambitious men for mounting to the consul-ship; the consulship, by the help of the military power, which in Rome it always implied, could easily be prolonged into a dictatorship for life; and this was only a pleasant name for a perpetual despotism. Of the prominent men who availed themselves of this democratic engine to destroy the liberties of their country, Marius, Pompey, and Julius Cæsar were the most prominent. Marius, a rough, rude, and uncultivated soldier to whom the overthrow of a shaggy Gaul as unmannerly as himself, or the bearding of a reverend senator fenced round by every form of law, was a work of equal delight, provided it afforded scope to his energy and fuel to the restless fire of his ambition ; Pompey, a man as a soldier more fortunate than brave, as a democratic leader more plausible than forcible ; and Cæsar, who to the vigour of a great soldier and the unscrupulousness of a thorough demagogue added the manners of a gentleman, the intellect of a statesman, and the attitude of a king. Commencing life as a champion of the people, and pushing himself into popularity by all those acts of courting the multitude and galling the nobility, which at Rome were practised as a trade, this great man had only to wait for the blunders of his less able competitors, and vigorously to use them. By the favour of the people he received the decennial command of those armies, which he speedily used for robbing them of their liberty. In all this he acted according to the highest standard of personal virtue, no doubt most falsely and most selfishly, but for the situation of affairs not unwisely. Nearly a century of feverish faction and sworded violence had made the once admired balance of the stable Roman polity like the memory of a dream. There was no peace now to be looked for in the regular way ; no order, no law. Democracy had done its perfect work, and was happy if its own minister clad with irresponsible power might lay the demons which its own conjurings had raised. A civilized servitude was at all events better than a sanguinary freedom.

PRUSSIA.

We now pass by a single leap across the vast chasm of centuries from ancient Rome to modern PRUSSIA, in order to present to our imaginations a well-marked type of a purely monarchical form of government. What the classical nations of antiquity combined to reject, and in their circumstances would likely have found impossible, a well ordered government under an absolute kingship, that modern Europe has realized in Prussia with the most distinguished success. In estimating the capabilities of this form of government however we must bear in mind that the Prussian power is of too modern a date to justify any very large conclusions with regard to the permanency of its political constitution, and that, in the shape of a reaction from the terrible blow of the battle of Jena, in 1806, it has already received into its autocratic body a certain infusion of the democratic spirit of the age which takes it out of the category of pure monarchy. We may define the Prussian polity therefore, since 1806, as an absolute monarchy, guided by the intelligence and qualified by the democratic spirit of the eighteenth century. Certain it is, however, that it has grown up rapidly to its present magnitude and importance chiefly under monarchical influences of the most unqualified character. The formal date of the reception of Prussia into the sisterhood of European monarchies, was the 18th of January, 1701 ; but the real commencement of the central vigour and power of growth which has characterised this kingdom was the battle of Fehrbellin, gained by Frederick William, the Great Elector, over the Swedes in the year 1675. In estimating the causes of the growth of a great nation much no doubt is due to the fortunate epiphany of the right man at the right time and the right place:

nevertheless, it is quite certain that some forms of government present greater facilities than others for the exercise of great political talents ; and in this view it seems unquestionable that Prussia owes more of her present elevation to her absolute form of government than to any other circumstance. Great kings, assisted by a ministry of skilful men, unmoved by the violence of democratic faction, and undistracted by the confusion of popular councils, have made Prussia. The lesson to be learned from her short and brilliant career is, that a strong central power—such a power as in this country would appear the most intolerable despotism—worked by a well-calculated machinery of intellectual dexterity—what they call a bureaucracy—can achieve results in the sphere of social organism which the most vigorous free constitution may look upon with envy. If rapid growth, skilful organisation both material and moral, and steadily mounting ascendancy be in any way connected with a particular form of government, the absolute monarchy of Prussia has as great a virtue to produce these results as the unlimited democracy of America. The assertion of the position of a young upstart kingdom by Frederick the Great, in the seven years' war against the combination of three of the most formidable European powers, was a much greater feat than the victories achieved by Washington over Earl Cornwallis, which gave independence to the American states in the year 1783. In popular education, in general intelligence, and in the culture of the most cosmopolitan learning, the monarchical Prussians have for three generations been the leaders of Europe ; and the signal blow which, with a celerity, a precision, and an effect worthy of the great Napoleon, they lately inflicted on their old rival, Austria, was the fruit altogether of a monarchical foresight, bureaucratic skill, and a professional firmness such as democratic councils rarely exhibit. That the Prussian government, therefore, has been in some views a great success, and that its name stands on the records of time as a striking proof of the political virtue of an intelligent despotism, no well-informed person can deny. I imagine Xenophon and Plato, whom the open vices of demagogy at Athens threw into a general habit of scarcely justifiable admiration for the aristocratic polity of Lacedæmon, would have found something much more suitable to their tastes as cultivated Athenians in the literary absolution of Potsdam and the scientific despotism of Berlin. On the other hand we must bear in mind, as already remarked, that had it not been for the fiery ordeal of Jena and Eylau which, under the guidance of Stein and Scharnhorst, resulted in the infusion of a strong popular element into the Prussian military organisation, the Prussian monarchy might, in the great German struggle, now in the process of completion, have been weighed in the balance and found wanting. We must never forget that the political successes of the late Bohemian campaign were due as much to the popular remodel of the materials of the Prussian army originating with Scharnhorst, as to the perfection of the monarchical machinery so skilfully handled by Bismark. The history of Prussia, therefore, proves no less manifestly than that of Rome, that whether king or aristocracy be the governing power, no government can achieve anything without the help of a willing people, whom the constitution of the country allows to feel their individual importance ;

and, in all probability, the parliamentary element recently introduced into the governmental machinery at Berlin, increasing, as it did in this country after the great civil war, with fresh accessions of power in every generation, will, before long, prove that an absolute monarchy even when administered with the greatest amount of intelligent insight, and paternal consideration, has become impossible in modern Europe, wherever the people are determined to assert their share in the government, or have not learned by a series of bloody defeats to despair of themselves, and to accept humiliation as the necessary price of repose.

AMERICA.

From the type of an unmixed monarchy on the banks of the Spree, let us now turn to that of an unmitigated democracy beyond the Atlantic. Here, however, though brilliant results are trumpeted, there is less material for making any sound deductions with regard to the mere form of government than even in Prussia. It is certain, no doubt, that America has prospered wonderfully ; but so has Victoria prospered, and so has New Zealand ; so has Glasgow in the northern, and Manchester in the southern division, of this busy island ; and, the present constitution of America, dating no further back than 1789, it were as absurd to pronounce a judgment on its governmental capabilities now as to decide the character of a man before he has passed the brilliant perils of puberty, or to prophecy the result of a long voyage when the good ship has scarcely left the land behind. The extravagant strain of laudation in which a certain class of politicians have been forward to eulogise the American polity must proceed either from the partiality of excited partisanship, or from the hastiness of that logic which cannot distinguish concomitants from causes, or from a natural reaction against that lust of depreciation in which not a few English writers have indulged when descanting on the peculiarities of American private and public life. All that Mr. Goldwin Smith and others have written eloquently in vindication of American institutions may be accepted gratefully as the refutation of the partial views and the extreme assertions of ultra conservative writers in this country ; as a commendation of pure democracy to a people living under the more happy system of a mixed monarchy, they seem to me altogether worthless. In fact, no person has denounced the fundamental vice of the democratic constitution of America in stronger terms than Mr. Goldwin Smith. Hear what he says about the Presidency in his late essay, one of a collection of democratically-tinted discourses on political matters recently published by Macmillan :—" The elective " Presidency, with its patronage, has always been the grand incentive of "faction, intrigue, and corruption ; and the hope of obtaining it has " been the greatest cause of obliquity in the courses of public men." This sentence brings to view a principle of moral corruption which belongs not only to the election of the President in America, but in a certain degree to the exercise of democratic functions of government even under the most favourable circumstances. If the majority of men were wise, good, independent, impartial, and cool enough to elect their best men for their highest public offices, then democracy would be the best form of government. But the case is quite otherwise. All popular elections are in their nature more or less tumultuous, beating with a feverish rather than a healthy pulse, and apt to be inspired by local prejudice rather than by large patriotism, by party passion more than by impartial reason. Moreover, politics is not a field in which the best and noblest men will, except under favourable circumstances, be eager to put forth their energies. Power, place, and pence, the natural rewards of political influence, are supremely desired, not by the best always, but often by the worst, members of the community; and accordingly, in every purely democratic country, where politics, as in America, becomes a trade, it is found that politicians are among the lowest and most worthless class of the community. Not the purest and the noblest rush into that scramble; mere power has no charm for a man who knows the blessedness of the higher inspiration which proceeds from a love of excellence; and, besides, even those whose natural genius fits them specially for public life, are repelled by their righteous aversion to that machinery of flattery, intrigue, slander, corruption, and juggle of all kinds, which are the common instruments of influencing the masses under a purely democratic constitution. The consequence is that an election in America is often the triumph of the most unprincipled and unscrupulous men over the most high-minded and the most virtuous; and a triumph achieved by the agency of the most vile, venal, and brutish elements of the community. Pure democracy, indeed, in modern America, as in the latter days of the Roman republic, has proved itself to be only a grand machinery for debauching the public conscience. No doubt, as compared with Rome, America has one advantage; it has no oligarchy planted by the constitution in direct hostile attitude to the people. But experience has taught that when the excited masses of a democracy have no aristocracy to quarrel with they will breed factions amongst themselves; and already, by the violence of party, we have seen the fervid young commonwealth torn into two, and a total sunderance prevented only by a civil war of the fiercest intensity, and the establishment of martial law in the subjugated half of the once free commonwealth. One danger incident to all democratic federations the infant republic has thus escaped—the danger of being split into a number of separate and independent states. The other danger remains, of annihilating local liberty by the increasing arbitrary authority of the great democratic Congress assembled at Washington. Of the tendency of this body to violence and interference there is sufficient evidence before the world; but it is always hopeful to think that the people in that part of the world have sometimes a great deal more sense and a great deal more dignity of character than the politicians who speak for them. There are also certain checks to popular insolence in the American constitution, as it stands on paper, which, if it is allowed fair play or practice, may retard, if they do not prevent, the establishment of that despotism which is the natural fruit of all democracy. I mean, of course, the senate, or upper house, the president, and the high position and supreme sanction of the law. These checks, however, as experience has proved, are not of such a nature as to be able to stand against the assaulting force of hot-spurred faction. Every preponderant power, whether monarchical, aristocratic, or democratic, is naturally tyrannical in its tendencies, and will always struggle to be tyrannical in its operations. The future efficiency of the constitutional checks, therefore, against popular excess in America, so cunningly forged by Alexander Hamilton, will depend principally on the moderation and good sense of the people; or rather—and here lies the danger—of their politicians; for we may understand by inference, even in this country, that the violence of demagogues, the antagonism of party leaders, and the general complexity of the parliamentary situation, may lead a house of representatives to pass measures of which the moderate and sensible part of the nation do not approve. To assert the unity, and at the same time maintain the freedom, of such a vast aggregate of federated states as America, must prove a Herculean task; and we cannot but wish our transatlantic cousins success in their attempt to solve a social problem on the large scale, which has as yet enjoyed only a very partial solution on the smallest scale. Looking at the past experience of the world we may justly refuse to be very sanguine in our expectations, much less dream of allowing ourselves to be led into the delusion of choosing their tentative form of government as a standard model for improving our own; but while to exult prophetically in the success of democracy in America would be to show too much confidence in man, to despair of it altogether would be to have too little faith in God. Our present business, therefore, with regard to America is to look and learn and be soberminded, waiting to see whether out of that huge vat of popular ferment shall be produced wine or vinegar.

ENGLAND.

After the above strictures on five peculiar types of polity, your own good sense will not have failed to make the implied inference with me, that the one which remains, our British constitution, is the best of all the six; and it is the best precisely because it contains within itself all the three elements that naturally belong to a complete social organism, one or the other of which it has been the misfortune of the other five to reject. The mixed constitution of this country presents in happy combination the unity and the loyal grace which belong to a monarchy, the stability and order which are characteristic of an aristocracy, and the energy and the propulsive power which are the soul of a republic. It is a constitution founded on a wise distrust of any single unlimited social power, and a safe confidence in the equalizing virtue of opposite pressures. There is a class of intellects in whose view this complex system of checks and balances possesses no value. These are minds generally of great vigour and intensity, but without breadth, and utterly incapable of appreciating the principle of rich variety on which God has created the world. Endowed with a transcendental faith in themselves, and an imperious instinct of self-assertion, persons of this type ride on with the assured conviction that the only hindrance in the way of a political millenium is whatsoever prevents them from having the reins altogether in their own hands. With them one-sidedness is excellence, and the exclusion of an opposite the ideal of perfection. But those who with a large sympathy and a penetrating eye, have looked into the deeper springs of physical or social organism, have learned a different doctrine. They have been instructed that health, and virtue, and all excellence, consist in the balance of extremes, the harmony of opposites, and the union of apparent incompatibles. This is the doctrine which Plato and Aristotle more than two thousand years ago, expounded in weighty prose, which Goethe, Wordsworth, and Tennyson, in our own days, have chiselled in elegant verse, and which forms, indeed, part of the current proverbial wisdom of all nations advanced a little beyond sheer barbarism. But in politics as in religion, nothing is more easy than to forget in practice maxims which are almost too stale to be preached on. No man of extreme democratic opinion, whatever he may profess, can have any real value for the British Constitution. He does not believe in moderation; his impatience is embittered by every check; and his insolence spurs him on to pluck the beard of every authority in the state which sets a bound to his intolerant dictation. But if this overpowering violence of the one-sided democratic politician is far removed from political wisdom, it behoves us to consider seriously at the present moment whether the most recent Reform movements in this country may not have been conducted in a manner, and may not be tending to results which will seriously endanger the permanence of our long-tried mixed form of government. A single glance at the history of the last three hundred years will show us, if we are not altogether blind, where the political danger of the present moment lies. Before the revolution of 1688 the kingly element preponderated in our constitution: up to the Reform Bill of 1832 the aristocratic element : since then the democratic element has asserted itself strongly, and is steadily on the increase. I am not one of those who have the slightest objection to this course of development. On the contrary, I admire it, in every view, as most rational, and rejoice in it as most successful. But it is manifest we have now reached a point where, if we do not use great caution and circumspection, in the heat of fervid pursuit, we run a great danger of losing at one wing of the battle what we have gained at the other. In 1832 we gained an immense advantage by bringing in the middle classes, as a salutary counterpoise to the upper classes and the aristocracy. From that moment our constitution entered on a new phasis; and we launched on a more brilliant, it may be, but, doubtless, also on a more perilous career. The danger now to be guarded against is neither monarchy, as in the days of Charles I., nor aristocracy, as at the commencement of the present century, but democracy. I do not mean to say, of course, that the Reform Bill of 1832 was a perfect, or could in any sense be regarded as a final measure. But I do say that in all succeeding Reform Bills, the prominent rock a-head which a wise state-pilot had to look out for was democracy. One great defect of that bill, undoubtedly, was that it enfranchised by the arbitrary line of a £10 rental, two classes of persons, of which those immediately below the line could not but feel in many cases, that they were equal if not superior in social value to those immediately above it. In a representative constitution no class of independent and respectable citizens, whether high or low in the scale should be entitled to complain that they are not represented. An expansion of the Reform Bill of 1832, therefore, became necessary.

But it did not by any means follow that to admit to the franchise any class previously excluded, necessarily implied a second dose of Reform on the purely democratic principle of ancient Athens and modern America. A strong measure in 1867, of Reform, exactly in the same direction as that in 1832, could not but disturb very seriously that balance of parties on which the very existence of constitutional government depends. If a process of this kind were to go on we could not but fall ultimately, under a despotism of mere numbers; quality would everywhere yield to quantity; and in the violent struggle for democratic supremacy, the government of the country would fall into the hands of those who were most ready to flatter the prejudices, and to magnify the wisdom of the multitude. It is easy to call this an imaginary picture; but the course of Roman history which I sketched above, under slightly different forms, foretypes the changes which we may naturally be destined to run through. It must be borne in mind that we have to deal in this country, and in this age, with the very same elements which made democracy so formidable in the later history of republican Rome, I mean an aristocracy and a plutocracy of enormous wealth, and right alongside of them a democracy of great energy, of little culture, and of extreme poverty. In such circumstances should the House of Commons by the Reform Bills now projected, or by others that may come after them, be so controlled, by a one-sided democratic spirit, as to bring our House of Commons into direct antagonism with our House of Lords, then the doom of our constitution is sealed. We may not have a civil war, perhaps, as in the days when Marius and Sylla headed alternately the democratic and aristocratic butcheries in ancient Rome; but we shall have certainly extreme counsels and violent measures, and the field cleared for a military despotism whenever the factions shall not be able to get on without a master. If our constitution is destined to last, it can only be by maintaining firmly the aristocratic element in the House of Commons, the existence of which alone guarantees our safety from a fatal clash betwixt the two most powerful organs of constitutional authority. It is for this reason that a Reform Bill at the present stage of our history, while it enfranchised the skilled artizan class, should at the same time have done something to give a real and not merely a nominal representation to the upper classes of many of our large towns. Wisdom also demanded that a reasonable substitute should have been provided for the loss of the small boroughs, the practical utility of which has been acknowledged by some of our greatest statesmen. But the demands of wisdom, which speak audibly in the room of the quiet thinker, are not readily heard amid the tumultuous hubbub of contending parties; and the measures of Reform which are proposed by practical politicians depend not less on what will be accepted than on what should be given. The unreasonable element in this region very often manages to control the reasonable; and even Solon, the most independent of all Reformers, after finishing the great work committed to him, was obliged to confess that he had given the Athenians not the best laws, but the best of which they were capable. I have often thought also, observing the blindness of great bodies of men to what is demonstrably for their benefit, that after a certain lease of existence, churches and states, like individual men, become incapable of receiving a new idea. If so, they must even go on as they have started, come to blossom and fruitage in the one-sided way of which they are capable, and perish in the unbridled excess of their pet excellence. But, however this may be, states, like individuals, if they wish to live long, should take care not to live too fast; and the more spirited a steed is the less need is there for a spur, and the more for a bridle. Whatever changes in our electoral system may be made by Whig or Tory ministers, the safety of the country is likely to depend much less on the particular form of the measure framed than on the moderation and sober-mindedness of the people ; and this we may most assuredly say, that the more democratic a form of government becomes the more public intelligence and virtue does it demand in the people, and the greater is the danger to which the social machine is exposed from the very potency of the steam by which it acts.

The talented Lecturer on resuming his seat was greeted with loud and repeated plaudits.

Mr. W. AMBROSE (barrister-at-law) proposed a vote of thanks to Professor Blackie for his able and very interesting lecture. It should be remembered that what the professor had stated was not the opinions and the language of a mere politician, but the experience and results of the study of political philosophy; and he was quite sure, considering that at this time the constitution of the country was about to undergo some change, it was most important that the great facts of history which had been explained that evening should be well understood by all who were called upon to remodel the constitution. (Hear, hear.)

CAPTAIN SAWYER seconded the vote of thanks, and expressed his conviction that the Constitutional Association, by such meetings as that, and the one recently held at the Corn Exchange, would prove of immense importance, and very materially increase the true Conservative principles of the Government. (Applause.)

Professor BLACKIE, in acknowledging the vote of thanks, which was carried amidst the greatest cheering, said it was not without trepidation that he stood upon the platform, but he thought that he was in the way of duty, and after it was done he thought it was pleasant to him if it was to them. (Hear, hear.) As to what had been said about professors leaving their sanctums, he thought it would be better for the professors if they did come out of those sanctums, and bring with them practical sympathy with the larger and more popular body of their fellow citizens. (Applause.)

Dr. ROYLE proposed a vote of thanks to Mr. C. Turner, M.P., for his courteous conduct in the chair. This country was now passing through one of what might perhaps be the most eventful and trying times of her history, and he believed that a great and glorious reformation would be much facilitated by what they had heard that evening—the result of great thought, labour, and industry on the part of the professor. There had been nothing said by Dr. Blackie that would influence the passions or excite the prejudices of any man, but he had calmly and dispassionately appealed to the reason of his audience in endeavouring to make them more fit to discharge the duties which the glorious constitution imposed upon them. Dr. Royle passed a very high eulogium upon Mr. Turner for the attention he paid both to the general interests of the country and the special interests of his constituents, and remarked that the hon. gentleman had that evening added another to the list of deep obligations owing from them.

Mr. Councillor ANDERTON seconded the motion, and expressed a hope that Mr. Turner would be able to return to his duties in London, strengthened by what he had listened to that evening, to counteract the feeling and opinions expressed by the junior member for South Lancashire—(applause)—and to show not only to that hon. gentleman, but to his friend John—(laughter)—that they were not all Radicals even in Manchester. (Hear, hear.)

Mr. W. R. CALLENDER, jun. (president of the association), who had taken the chair previous to the vote of thanks being moved to Mr. Turner, endorsed all that had been said of that gentleman, who not only thought right, and when he addressed the House of Commons spoke right, but also voted right; and who was one of the majority who on Saturday morning week affirmed the principle on which he (Mr. Callender) believed a just and fair Reform Bill could only be based—household suffrage, coupled with proper residence and personal payment of rates. (Hear, hear.) As he had not been able to address a meeting of the Constitutional Association before, owing to his absence from town, he perhaps might be permitted to express his regret at not being able to attend the meeting at the Corn Exchange some weeks since, nor of being present with the deputation which called lately upon the Chancellor of the Exchequer in Downing-street, which he believed had materially strengthened the hands of the Government. (Cheers.) He hoped that meeting would be an earnest of what they should have for the future, and that the Constitutional Association would become the centre of many Conservative associations in South Lancashire. He hoped too that when another election took place those who had been befooled last time by Mr. Gladstone's proclivities in former times would, fearless of him or his allies, vote in such a manner as would enable Mr. Egerton and Mr. Turner to have a colleague which would faithfully and truly look after, not only the private and public, but the general political interests of the constituency. (Applause.)

The vote of thanks to Mr. Turner, M.P., was passed unanimously, and in returning thanks the hon. gentlemen, after expressing his pleasure at attending the meeting and at hearing the excellent lecture, said he could confirm Mr. Callender's statement that the recent deputation from the Conservatives of Lancashire was of essential service to, and felt to be so by, the Government, and would tend much to counteract the democratic principles of those who were bent upon undermining the constitution.

Three cheers were given for Lord Derby, Mr. Disraeli, and the Government, and the proceedings terminated.

www.ingramcontent.com/pod-product-compliance
Lightning Source LLC
Chambersburg PA
CBHW021610270326
41931CB00009B/1406